Sonnets

Also by David Novak:

Sonnets

DAVID NOVAK

NON FIT PRESS
CHICAGO, ILLINOIS

Library of Congress Catalog Card Number: 99-85861

ISBN: 0-9675429-4-4

Printed in the United States of America

10 9 8 7 6 5 4 3 2 1

Contents

viii

That Our Lord Jesus died upon the cross
I must affirm, although it is denied
By many, whose denial is their loss,
For in the soul of man, I know he died:
He died, and ever-dying must out-live
The longest exhalation of sad breath,
Who came to teach rude mankind to forgive
And also, by the bye, refuted death.
Lord Jesus, Jesus, Lord, the Word is thee,
The Word made flesh, and flesh forever free
From its constraint of petty profiteering,
Forever to endure, though words may pass,
Confute, confound, perplex the mind from hearing,
From calling and recalling, what He was.

Evacuate me from this weary realm
When Thou hast worked Thy will in me, dear Lord,
Then lay my body in a grove of elm
By men to be remembered, or ignored;
While squirrels scamper to collect their hoard,
And wild dogs frolic under autumn skies
As daylight turns to dusk, and sound unheard
Each falling leaf in brilliant splendor dies;
While men and women exculpate their sighs,
Commemorating briefly with a pause
Their buried dead, who live in memories
Maintained by the comport of human laws;
Our dreams and hopes, like sweepers, come to
    naught—
Then leave each private paucity forgot.

That thou art gone—what, shall I weep for thee
That wast not, for a moment, ever true,
And friendly counsel that was given me
Not heeded, in the way that lovers do?
That thou art gone away—what, shall I weep
That thou, the cause of sorrow, hast departed;
Though memories run silent, and stay deep
In man's heart's core, when man is broken-hearted.
Art thou the selfsame bitch that Shakespeare loved,
Thou Beatrice turned strumpet ere the day
On Dante's love hath set, who was reproved,
Helen with lusty Paris run away?
Despite great pain, I have been grateful to
The Source to which all gratitude is due.

Gratitude? Ay, and grateful more in this
Despite great pain, of passion unrequited,
That love was ever, and my birthright is,
Ere thou wast born, who Adam's first-love slighted.
Love is time's hussy, ample and spread-eagle
That meets her mates, and then devours her prey
Although her face is fair, and manner regal,
And Him reduces to a senseless clay.
Think you my words are false? Then have it so;
For ever fools will cling to falser truth
Until their ravishment accedes to woe
And tyrant Age usurps the throne of Youth.
This, did you ever read the Master's sonnet
    You'd know, and more; yea, Shakespeare wrote
        upon it.

Let this, then, be my monument—for what?
Young man that followest, heed not this place,
Nor mourn the Poet here whose hope was cut
Early, and later fell to his disgrace.
Think not on us, thy predecessors, Poet
If Poet true thou art; think not on us,
For thou shalt feel whet-bladed sorrow, know it,
That gut-engourging time begot on us.
My Brother, this thy destiny and shame,
So greatly blest in love that love should pale
Beside what thou hast tasted, pure love's flame
That makes the conscience flicker, spirit fail,
And even words abandon thee for now
Before the great, unconscionable Thou.

David, ay David loved his Bonnie once,
Wherefrom his choicest sorrows emanate;
What love did turn a boy into a dunce
And all his better powers ruinate.
So long ago; now *mezzo di cammin*
He stops and waits, and wonders of love's future,
Vast ages hence: what do our passions mean
Except some wound the doctor has to suture?
The pity in the pain, the pain the passion;
Ye English poets, Wilfred Owen, Keats,
What now, when language no more is the fashion,
What now, Millay, and William Butler Yeats?
To write for ay, what has been better writ,
Again, again—where is the end of it?

The Friendship House, they made a home for thee
These many years ago, in thy "decline,"
Last years of illness, and of penury,
Though wanting neither love, nor weed, nor wine.
Decline? No, not decline in spirit ever,
Though thy sad life we never did support,
The opportunity now gone forever;
But thou wast wise, and had thine own purport.
What times were they? And what, again, are these?
America, far from thy native land,
Embraces thee—fulfills thy prophesies,
Her gaudy treasures sinking in the sand.
To thee, whose verse exceeds the choicest wines,
Dear Claude McKay, I dedicate these lines.

My only wish, which I may not attain,
Years hence when my poems bound and printed are
That I may have an introduction written
For them like what Max Eastman wrote for thine,
So generous and sweet, so full of care,
Wherefore "the mind was wrung, the pencil bitten,"
Instead of some encomium more fine,
Sententious in its praise, to pay for pain.
This I may never have; because my life
Lacks all the grace and generosity
Of thine, dear Claude. In meanness pass my days,
Each than the last more odious to me,
And fever-fits no spoken word allays
But plunge me further headlong into strife.

It's scarcely recognized that Claude McKay
Of all the poets of his generation
Except for Wilfred Owen, wrote the best
(And he Jamaica born!) iambic line,
Pentameter of pleasant modulation,
While this and that, like Eliot, professed
It an outmoded fashion, like some wine
"Not suited for the taste of present day."
But so it goes; and look at the successors
Of Eliot—their verse is all a mess!—
No fault of his, all mutually admiring
Each other's spewage, calling it "finesse,"
And "poetry" and "verse," the lot conspiring
To keep the lie concealed from their assessors.

To "tell the ancient tale," but "make it new,"
This is the Poet's task; what he has done
Since ancient time, and must forever do
Until on humankind sets its last sun.
I mine my ancient grief, my ancient love,
The vast disaster and defeat of all
My forces marshalled trying to disprove
Harsh legends of the great Sea's jealous thrall.
The Sea of Love, that spares not man nor whelp
Who undertakes the journey 'cross its breast,
And wracks them, heeding nary calls for help,
Sobs of remorse, regret, nor all the rest.
But thou hast overwhelmed my humble bark,
And I am all alone, and it is dark.

By all my friends forsaken, more or less,
But left to ruminate, "upon my ruin,"
The wastage and debris behind me strewn
Do I survey, as ever on I press;
Onward, from darkness into darkerness,
Nurtured despair my one and only boon
As with it I my loneliness festoon,
For no one heeds a man in his distress.
The soft caress, soft word that might have come
To change it, now could only come too late,
For I insensate am, struck blind and dumb,
As all against her kind I nurse my hate.
And yet, I can't deny that she was fair,
Although untrue, and sweet beyond compare.

Let there be commerce, then, between us, Love,
As that Old Poet said. Let us be friends:
Our injuries the consequences of
Too great a passion. Let us make amends.
Thus said, our love renew to former state,
Of fresh tranquility, and life restore
To peaceful days as we have known of late
And to such bounty as we had before.
Our time may pass ere long. Say we have quibbled,
My wrongs and thine, no more to linger on;
My former words forget, a somewhat ribald
Effusion made, when maidens will be won.
Old jealousy consigned to banishment
For now, let us replenish our content.

Shakespeare, forgive the wrong I do thy lyric
In echoing thy verses in my lines,
My crude attempts enough to give an earache
To thee long buried; vulgar anodynes.
How can thy influence on me diminish
When thy own sonnets taught to me my trade,
Though till my days of versifying finish
I cannot hope a something as well-made.
Vulgar attempts of piecemeal sloppiness
My verses are, the lot not unified,
Reflective of my life—I but digress
From that high standard thou hast dignified.
Such is my lot; but let it be confessed,
If mine are not so good, they are my best.

What, shall I go to her when thou art here?
The thing I said was said without my thinking
Of what it meant, or when it reached your ear
Would mean to thee—I didn't have an inkling.
My ignorance, that is the whole of me
Not learned in those refinements used to woo you
By other men, except the soul of me
And that so long ago was given to you.
Given for you to take or to forsake,
It matters not, so take it as a gift
Or let it drop, and into pieces break,
Between thy yea or nay there is no rift,
For I have made my choice, and given it
For you to mortify, or else enliven it.

Jesus, I cannot worship thee the way
A priest would have me worship—thou art far,
So far from me, and I am *senza fe,*
Except thou knowest, for a nearer star.
Let me inside his great faith cloakéd be,
As men may lose themselves inside a cause,
Worshipping him this side idolatry,
Thy saint and pilgrim, who discerned thy laws,
And then, his journey done, lived out his days
In exile from that city much accursed
By Florentines; and now has passed from praise
Into his greater glory, as he durst.
Like as the Sufi master, I can't be
Thy friend; but friend of this great friend of thee.

"Think ye the Word exists in Arabic?
We speak in ways that ye may understand!
Think ye the Faith is but some conjurer's trick,
Consigned to chosen tongue, or blood, or land?
Woe be to they who in their hearts believe
That prophesy has ended, like the Jews
In ancient times; nor shall they slightly grieve
If any sent by Me they should refuse.
Last Prophet? Fools! Look to the ancient scripture,
'All things are possible to Me' which saith;
As Jonah knew, nor can ye ever capture
My Will to peg to some tight-fitted faith!
Go back and read again!" This a voice spoke,
The night replete with dreams, when I awoke.

"As if Muhammad quarrels with Jefferson,
Or Sakya Muni Krishna did deride;
The truth is here before you, every one:
'Tis hard to understand? Well then, decide.
Why else this faculty, facility
Of mind was given to you, if not to
Investigate Me independently,
But to explore, my sacred Will to do.
Where is the conflict here, except inside
The soul of vain hypocrisy and lies,
A fissure in the soul the light denied
As Judas did, and any who denies.
The pure in heart, Our mercy goes to them,
But traitors, cowards, quislings We condemn!"

Father, because I hope to have Thy blessing
In hopes for which I hope Thou canst approve,
My paltry sins I must go on confessing,
But not the greater one: that I do love.
Herself she gave to me, so great a bounty,
Which taking, I became her humble slave;
Not registered in any state or county,
The world may never know what love we have.
A love that's closest to insanity
Although approved, and sanctioned by the law,
Not vain, although it is a vanity
Of near-perfection, not without its flaw,
Which she and I detect. The rarest gems
Have flaws; from flaws the rarest beauty stems.

Thou jade against the windowsill, has my
Neglect caused this, thy leaves all drooped and
   dropping?
For want of water have thy veins gone dry,
Or was my bigger plant thy sunlight stopping?
Or just the opposite—hast thou been scorched
By this year May's unseasonable hot?
No, like as not, thou art for water parched,
An' though it come too late, here is a shot.
There, there, sweet plant, pray do not go the way
Of that old Basil that once set beside thee,
Rememberest that far, that somber day
When from thy former friend did fate divide thee?
Too busy have I been my love attending,
Which like thine own sad life, may now be ending.

Nor not against the lathe of heaven run,
Though many men will try, and thereby perish,
For though we finish having not begun,
Our memories of dreams we have to cherish;
Or else what is there, love, our whole life living,
To make the loss of it have been worthwhile,
Unless the empty promise of our striving
Shall clutter up a corner in a pile.
Useless effects, and promises unkept
Shall our unbidden devastation spread
Into the secret corner where we slept
And now pollute the very marriage bed?
The subterfuge of lust, and sacrilege
Now sack and sacrifice our heritage.

Wert thou not here, then would I go to her,
For comfort in my aching weariness,
Or would I heed the heat of passion's spur
Into the night's abysmal dark recess?
Along the wharves, become a denizen
Of that dark world, where gaudy pleasure's trade
Surfeits the most assiduous of men
As passion's quest is endlessly replayed?
Or would I but retreat into some place
Where I might build a shrine to thee, in mind,
And meditate upon the lovely grace
That in thy face I was the first to find?
These all I've done, in contemplation queer
Of what I'd do tonight, wert thou not here.

"The poetry I write is what I read"
Wrote Robert Service, and I go with him,
In our technique and aims we are agreed,
Though scholars scowl his poetry to skim;
The cackle of the geese and barnyard fowl
Preferred to eagles soaring overhead,
The lesser poets, this was his avowal,
Instead of those Great Mighty Masters dead.
Longfellow too, and many more besides—
You have to trust your heart, the reputation
Bestowed by scholars bald are but asides,
Tools to secure their own self-preservation.
Cummings or Service, honest craftsmen all,
With ye my brethren, do I stand or fall.

O ho! somebody make a point to keep
A book by Ginsburg (it'll disappear
Most silently into the vasty deep
That claims our labor's fruits when we're not here),
Or any of the others, otherwise
People will never know what stuff you read,
America—who would believe their eyes,
To see what lies the people can be fed.
The whole long list of names, ye gads, remember!
The pomp and fuss that people made for them;
But even greatness simmers to an ember
And laureates forsake their diadem.
Press onward into all-engulfing night,
Ye poets, pundits, fools so erudite!

24

"Deliberate fiction" poetry or else
"Fictive deliberation"? Either way
If not in fact the truth it always tells
Expresses our experience today.
More precious is the light so faerily
That dances in your eyes, than any sonnet,
That all my verse I'd sunder cheerily,
And even Shakespeare's, just to gaze upon it.
To gaze upon it; but you have departed,
And rain beats on the panes so wild without;
Within my gloomy ritual has started,
Retracing pains that life is mild without.
Because we quarreled, you harshly slammed the door
Departing here, despite the mad downpour.

25

"More precious is the light," so wrote Millay,
Better than half a dozen poets not
Ever excluded, as she is today
From compilations, and her work forgot.
These are the scholars making their decisions,
Based on what motives, do you dare to ask,
Subjecting work that's good to rank derisions,
In glory mediocre stuff to bask.
These *hombres necios* is who they are,
Anthologists discretely shaping our
Legacy to the future, in their care,
Through ignorance or else abuse of power.
But we that know, we honor thee, Millay,
No matter what the *literati* say.

26

Yet children must have babysitters in
Their lengthy adolescence nowadays,
And so, to compensate for their chagrin,
Their teachers pay, but mostly pay with praise;
The honor and accord which is bestowed
To them as "poets," while they are at school,
Exchanging every ode and palinode
Amongst their peers, with whom there is no duel.
For praise they lavish one upon the other,
And write about each other's publications,
And write critiques implying one another
Has written work that's worth qualifications.
But here's the secret: people playing fools
And poetasters, aren't confined to schools.

All lack the secret: love. This I have found
In thee, all life and love demystifying,
A brief conjunction neither owned nor zoned,
These days we spend, my poor verse justifying.
What, have you gotten old? I cannot see it,
If time has "delved a parallel into
Thy brow," as so you say, why then so be it,
Myself I see it not, so why should you?
But I have gotten older, past my prime
By many years, and you'll seek other new men
Who can in other ways than meager rhyme
Accommodate your well-renowned acumen.
So let it be; but let us not be brief
In mischief-making, though it end in grief.

Father, my words may too in time disperse,
And surely will, according to Thy will,
But yet this love, which I set down in verse
I'll class a miracle, my death until.
Truly my skills are lacking, meager, dull;
Truly my words but falsify the truth
By making love seem empty that is full,
And in harsh grating sounds, though meant to soothe.
Forgive my inborn talent's bad misuse,
When I so little care devote to it,
My words but an affront to her my muse,
My passions passing in a startled fit.
Lord, let not now hypocrisy in verse
My efforts taint, and past success reverse.

Hast thou forsaken me forever, then,
My muse, the inspiration of my verse,
Because we quarreled? So shall we sever, then,
And all our happy memories reverse
In one fell swoop, and former blessings curse?
So be it then, although it heavily
On my head fall, because my blame is worse;
So shall my guilty sin bedevil me,
While thou, who early heardst the reveille
And warning call, hast quickly left me here;
But I, who acted nearly evilly
Can never seek my solace anywhere.
My muse, but thou canst turn my situation,
Forgiving me, and giving—inspiration!

30

"Poets write things in which they don't believe."
What does this mean? We don't believe in love?
We don't believe that Adam and that Eve,
Our ancient parents, heard a Voice above,
Telling them not to eat that apple of
Knowledge of right and wrong? No, none of these.
It means belief, which none of us may prove,
Is not our function: those are privacies,
Specific to the soul that waits release
From bondage to the body to its greater,
Lasting and uncommemorative peace,
That happens after death, and even later.
What poets don't believe in, meaning death,
Was proved fallacious ere they drew their breath.

"Pass to thy rendezvous of light," she wrote,
But madness was it, that "divinest sense,"
Which saved my life, a little dinghy, boat
With which I might traverse the vast immense.
So shall we thank our predecessors, then,
Who left behind them signs for us to follow?
Shall we exalt them higher than all men,
With praise to raise them though that praise be
    hollow?
What do they need from us? Not anything,
Except our strict observance of our duty,
Not in allegiance to an earthly king,
But Him above, Whose hidden face is beauty.
This we may do, with never need to tell
What early frost beheads our asphodel.

32

My friend, 'tis two long years since I have seen thee,
And yet, thou knowest, I am beholden to
Another, who hath placed herself between me
And this wide world, by being fair and true.
Her presence colors all my waking hours
Except when absence leaves me in despair,
My mistress, while the press of time devours
All honor, pride, because she's true and fair.
When present, all my thoughts are banished far
From every object, save her lovely face;
When absent, as consumed in mortal war,
My mind a battle wages with disgrace.
Then ceaselessly I work and live in strife,
Dishonoring my friends, and her—my life.

My meager talents, useless in her service,
Nor does she care a whit for what I write,
But mocks it—why, it makes a fellow nervous,
Though others may approve; and she is right.
Too fair for verse, yet verse is all I have;
Too true for words, and all that they conceal;
Too harsh for life, but not meant for the grave;
Too good for me, though making my life real.
So ever after her I take pursuit,
Her wordless beauty, striving still to capture,
But never catching up with her repute
Though even shadows cast from her enrapture.
What grace and charm, verse only intimates
Half-heartedly, and thus prevaricates.

34

These "hombres necios que acusáis,"
One of their lot am I, who bear my curse
And stigma with me, heart now made of ice,
Although I bare my soul's hard fate in verse.
Against her pleasant virtue obdurate,
Though other men may praise, and say how fair
That beauty is—which I have learned to hate—
That's formed her face, and learned to nestle there.
Hate because I naively put my trust
In sidelong glances that she cast at me,
Not knowing she would trample in the dust
My hope, nor lust enslave what had been free;
Not knowing that, when she leaned over to me,
And kissed and pressed, my heart would shoot right
    through me.

35

Why did I never hear the name before
Of such an honest painter, Horace Pippin,
When names like Ellsworth Kelly stir a roar
Of acclamation up, on exhibition?
This is America I've never seen
So accurately, or so well portrayed,
The facts of who we are and who we've been
On canvasses and panels so well-made.
Whose poetry evolved out of the war,
Painting I mean, where else does artistry
Arise but from such passioned pains that jar
Not mind, but soul from its tranquility.
War Wilfred Owen wrote about ere his
Own death a week before the armistice.

36

What do I know of art? Not anything;
So that when passers-by declare as crude
The half of it, I have no arguing,
Because I'd rather see an honest rude
That critics, skeptics, or the multitude
Dismiss for its technique, if it affirms
What truth I've witnessed and does not exclude
An aspect, and in no uncertain terms.
At base we mortal men are lowly worms
That have been given glimpses, though but rarely,
Of God's great glory, underneath which squirms
The pegged soul pinned to human squalor squarely.
These glimpses call out the artistic soul
To tell the truth blood-charged, but tell it whole.

37

Then shall I plumb the underworld, and seek
In shadows pleasures shadowy, and new,
Because you left, and now refuse to speak
To me, although my deep contrition's true.
Then let me seek tonight a rendezvous
With someone I have never met before,
Someone who's very different from you,
And who I'll never see, when it is o'er.
Tomorrow night another, and again
Still yet another, since you say to Hell
To me, and all my wasted hope have slain,
My misspent folly, loving you too well.
But yet if I could talk to you tonight,
Then all my darkness would be turned to light.

Dry days, dry days, my soul is parched with thirst
For love long absent, in these recent days'
Adversity, my last hope's bubble burst
By what took place; and left is a malaise
Of indecision, insecurity
Of whither, wherefore, how, and for what reason
To strive—*"ricorditi, ricorditi"*—
For what the soul has lost in its self-treason.
The memory of her, so far away,
What hope in my despair can it now offer
To linger on the memory today
When I have no obeisance left to proffer
In expiation or propitiation
To her, when I have failed in my temptation.

Torturous deprivation is my life,
My misfit days in misfit folly spent,
When I can hardly hold the fork and knife
To feed myself, or much less pay the rent.
Lord, what was done was done without consent,
My ignorance abused, my trust betrayed,
Hurling me to eternal discontent,
Myself to its self-banishment relayed.
Then is it any wonder I, dismayed,
So fiercely went afoul and went astray
In wake of what she wrecked, and what she made
Grow in its place, that tortures me today;
Long, long years after that sad heinous fact
Of what it was, that she did there enact.

"Submission to the will of God" is good,
Yet what the will of God is, none can say,
Though many people have it understood,
And gladly condescend to show the way.
"The Lord wills this", "the Lord wills that,"
    one hears,
As if they have a secret channel to
His innermost desire—their hopes and fears
As congruous with what He'd have them do.
"When Christians came, and brought the Bible, we
Possessed the land; but now we have the Bible,
They, the land"—wherefore servility
Is preached, and blasphemy a form of libel.
So Creeds have ever confiscated booty,
And yoked the dispossessed to heaven's duty.

The Great Crusades, re-taking what was taken,
In full approval of authority,
Yet neither side, in taking, was mistaken,
For as God wills, so must it come to be.
"The Lord wills this", "the Lord wills that,"
    destruction
Of every other temple than your own,
The sullen peoples lined up for induction
Into thy Creed, and sacred holy Zone.
Ay, labor for the Lord; and let thy labor
Reflect the honor of Who Doth Command,
Thy wealth, thy riches—property, good neighbor—
Consign to His, that is to say, my hand.
Then when the ink has dried, transaction sealed,
Great God, let not Thy mercy be repealed.

All I possess unto Thy grace redound,
Great palaces, and vistas, all to Thee
In Thy Name consecrated, by me owned .
But by the blessing Thou hast given me.
The blessing, Lord, of knowing Thee much better
Than other, heathen tribes, Thou one God only,
Allah, Jehovah, naming by the letter
The Law that raiseth me, and my sod only.
Me, me, dear Lord, that is the holy word,
Not "aum" as other people understand;
To me let all obeisance be conferred,
To me, devotion, and—what's better—land!
Me, me, Mosaic or Mohammedan,
Me, me, for Jubilee, for Ramadan!

My bent cantankerous, which made her leave me
Full rightfully, which leaving made me know
What I knew not, although the knowledge grieve me,
Relieve me of, dear Lord, and let me go
Forward—though never gaining what I want—
Most treasured lost what having never prized;
Though I my former words cannot recant,
Harsh speaking that was rank and ill-advised.
Lord, why, when love was held in my possession,
Devout, ripe, tranquil, as if meant for me
Only but I was caught in the obsession
Of bitter fruits that cannot ever be.
I let her fly to where she happy is,
Away from here, and my unhappiness.

Lithe limbs my limbs did once enfold,
Soft lips my lips did, parting, kiss,
Such grace as man may once behold
Then parting from, forever miss.
Sweet breath with my breath intermingled
As passion pressed us close together
In unison, as bodies tingled
Not knowing which was either neither.
Light-murmured words of deep import
As tuned my ear to their caressing,
As gentleness became our sport,
Gentility our only blessing.
Wild days of love, yet numbered few—
And since 'tis years, since I had you.

Soft-spoken, mild, obedient,
A good girl who believes in God,
Such was the blessing I was sent,
Who let me love her mind and bod.
She wasn't old but she was wise
In how a woman serves a man,
And gives him, not just sweetest eyes,
But her allegiance, as she can.
Devotion, Lord, and rites of passion,
As in the holy name fulfilled,
Not jealousy nor quest for fashion
To ever see his passion killed.
Forgive me, Lord, if it is wrong
For many loves as this to long.

Lord, if Thy will permits it please
Forgive my errors of the past,
And me to better days release
From misspent hopes and fears miscast.
Lord, if my body lets me have
The fairer sex to hold as mine
But as a lover, not a slave,
Obedient to things divine;
And if Thy will permits it, Lord,
A harem, and seraglio,
But pleasant, not some angry hoard,
Where I may keep my women so—
So let me, if Thou canst approve,
But let me not forsake Thy love.

Forgive me, God, if this is wrong,
But I believe it isn't so;
For I have had this passion strong
Since in my early days of woe.
But let Thy will be done, not mine,
And what I ask for never be
Unless with Thy intent divine
The hopes I have don't disagree.
I'd rather be a pauper poor
Devoid of even slightest ease
Than have fulfilled this wish and more
If with Thy will it disagrees.
Thy mercy, Lord, is all I ask,
To teach me to fulfill Thy task.

48

Lord, this I never had to ask
Did she, my older love, remain,
Without whom life's a loathsome task,
But full of sorrow, strife, and pain;
Had she been faithful, fair and true
Much as she promised me to be,
And not to do as women do,
Which I believed—so look at me!
My heart and soul to her I gave,
Naive because I loved too well
A person I might never have
Nor what we had must ever tell.
Wherefore, dear Lord, do I beseech
To compass loves within my reach.

49

Hast thou returned to me, my wanton muse,
To mock me after long, long years of pain,
To flirt with me again, then to refuse,
And so to set a madness in my brain?
Well then, I welcome thee if truly thou
To me returnest, and my crime forgotten
The former words we spoke to disavow
As something meager, petty, mean and rotten.
Love, let our old acquaintanceship renew
Itself like on the ashes of a fire
Long thought extinct, with effort tried and true
A bright new flame might thereupon suspire.
So, thou returnst to me, again I write;
But let me burn my former efforts trite.

Muhammad had no need of poetry,
Listen! nor Jesus need of native tongue
To carry each his message sea to sea,
Into the hearts of both the old and young.
For Jesus was the word that was made flesh,
Immutable, although in outward form
It manifestly change, forever fresh,
From tongue to tongue, to every tongue its norm.
The words Muhammad brought, no less remain
Without the need of poetry to prop them
In Arabic, although with greater pain
To sundry tongue translated not to stop them.
A moiety superfluous it is,
This poetry I write; nor ever wise.

Thou Jesus, Lord, how didst thou come to us
From our iniquity to liberate
As had the force and circumstantial fuss,
Us from the ancient bonds of greed and hate,
And usury, that canker-blot of sin
(Though men still draw their living in that way)
That approbation of the Sanhedrin
Did draw itself, until thou hadst thy say.
Yet men will kill on holy days, as said,
And prop for private benefice the words
As evidence of thy great wounds that bled
That thou hast left behind; their guilt engirds
Thy holy truth, to seminate instead
Lies to be fed on by rapacious birds.

To them the homosexuals give Thy
Conditional forgiveness, Lord, for they
Have had enough of hate and malice by
Their counterparts, the macho men, who stray
If not in any greater, in an equal
Though opposite direction, with their prancing,
So self-assured as if there were no sequel
To what each offered womankind, romancing.
God, I'm so sick of this! Americans
Like as obsessed with it, their human nature,
When everything is sex, and happenstance,
And fills the air with lively nomenclature.
A sensual life in moderation does
Nobody harm—don't misconstrue the laws!

53

Thou early blossomed flower of perfume sweet,
Than all our English poets high above,
So delicate, so true in line, complete,
Thou didst reveal for aye thy poet's love;
In lines upon the grecian urn, and on
A nightingale, "To Autumn," and the rest,
The goal near-winning, that was never won,
These are a handful, and they are the best.
Poet sublime! who speak the English tongue
That haven't known thy verse, are poor indeed,
Forever bountiful, forever young,
Singing of death forever "life's high mead."
In days of wasteful clatter, crash and glare,
To comprehend requires a palate rare.

Thou youthful flower, of "accidental power,"
Too early didst thou bloom, for thy own good,
But held to scorn by pundits of the hour
Deriding what they never understood.
Thou hast withstood them all, John Keats, and thou
Immortally in verse shall live while voice
Gives rise to English tongue, though even now
It suffers great abuse; but yet, rejoice!
Let us rejoice in thee, the erstwhile living,
Who carry in our hearts a glad memento
To cherish while we live, amidst great striving,
Pale England's best approach to quattrocento;
Verse-painting of such delicate refinement
As makes a panacea of confinement.

55

Fair youth beneath the trees, thou didst not live
To see the wanton, Fame, come after thee;
But, having learned thy measure, she could give
Pale sustenance to thy sad reverie.
Would I could be so steadfast! I had rather,
To have such fame, as Michelangelo
Did write of Dante, he who is my father,
The world's most splendid portion all forego.
The petty pleasures of this life, and gains,
Mean nothing! but to have that kind of honor
Posterity has paid thee for thy pains
Of my last comfort I would be the donor,
Accept obscurity, and lamentation,
Than like an Alexander, rule a nation.

On seeing thee, thou dark and passing fair
Despite a four year interval, it seems
Thou hast not changed, except perhaps thy hair,
The intervening time as lucid dreams;
But seeing thee again recalls back up
The passing words we had, of slight import,
And which I sipped as coffee from a cup,
Allegiance-tied, as conscience did exhort.
And I am quite beside myself, now watching
Thy fond familiar form about its motions,
Thy loveliness I had no hope of catching,
Now like a warship home to native oceans.
Yet I'll not play the conqueror discrete,
Having returned from wars, and great defeat.

"All's fair in love and war" the maxim goes,
Yet I have never seen it, though the force
Against us be unprincipled, and gross,
For scruple must remain our fighting's source,
Or all is lost. The ancients knew this well;
For great defeat is often as a masque
Concealing victory, while triumph's yell
Resounds most loudly in an empty cask.
The pompous conqueror in outward form,
Unschooled in liquid power's formlessness,
Doth oft neglect the calm within the storm,
And incremental change, though seeming less.
Such as was I, my sails puffed up with pride,
Full confident, until you left my side.

The image Dante had, of a ship's sails,
But such was I, puffed up and arrogant
As men will be, until such day as fails
Love's gentle breeze, and basis of their cant;
Such, such was I, by vain misattribution
According to myself what was my love's,
When I, an empty shell, my contribution
Is functional, like as a workman's gloves.
Useless am I, but love which channels through me
Subverts me to its means, until its end,
And then, as if it never even knew me,
Me shall discard like an unwanted friend.
This I accept, as to death happily
Do people march, possessed of such as she.

O she is fair, and true, and dangerous!
Let any who approach her, forewarned be
That though her countenance seem beauteous
There lurks behind great fury's cloudy see.
O, she is like the sky, still decorous
Surpassing normal days, foreboding soon,
In observation's training skilled to us,
Her poets and admirers, a typhoon;
Or, as the moment just before a quake,
Stillness pervades the soul, pervades the heart,
Then suddenly the world begins to shake,
So her great love, foundation of my art.
Now all is still; I wait and watch the clock,
Anticipating her next dreadful shock.

60

Then this is love? Young men, go seek it not.
No, better to stake out your hermitage
In some forsaken spot, with single cot
Than to be bowed to love that is the rage.
My warning this, though ye may never heed
(God, don't I know!) what our experience
Has taught to us to tell, who in our greed
To capture love gave up all innocence.
We old, our words seem folly to the young,
Until, unto their own decrepitude
They are matured, whereat the song as sung
By age strikes out in terror thrice renewed.
I never any more read poetry,
Since my life's utter change, she wrought in me.

"I will not cease from mental fight," he wrote,
To be a poet is to keep on fighting
Huge mental battles, but of little note
As scarcely intimated to in writing.
My battles I have fought, and largely lost,
My mental habits' disability
Increasing daily, at so large a cost
In effort to maintain stability.
"Shabby equipment," scarcely meant to deal
With these enormous clashes I am facing,
My vague attempts to ascertain what's real
Despite the errant patterns I've been tracing.
As life's incumbency demands a scheme,
As Blake declared, I'll make one from a dream.

My verse is like a scaffolding whereby
My soul I hope to rescue from perdition,
Although what I have witnessed, bye and bye,
But makes me doubt if I may see fruition
In this, my petty efforts of contrition
When largely looms inside a harsher bent
That forces me, against my best volition
And contrary to claims I'm innocent
That I have made, to see my best intent
Foiled, the charges brought by my accusers
Against me steeled seemless, and unbent,
Enough to make me one of the Refusers
Against my will, as often men accused
Forsake their right, to be by wrongs abused.

Lord, in my great disaster now unfolding,
Please let me see some signs of a reversal
Against the foe that ever I'm beholding
That has me beaten back, foe universal;
Against whom in an hour of dark distress
Before my eyes the heavens cleaved apart
To show the mechanism most men guess
Of thine unbending Justice—great Thou art.
And yet, in spite of this amazing grace
Revealed to me, I cower in despair,
Like as a child seeking mother's face
I call Thee, but Thou art not anywhere.
My lack of faith, dear Lord, preserve me from,
Though panic-stricken, all my calls are dumb.

These names I keep repeating, such as Keats
And Hopkins, part of the unique succession
Of poetry's transmission each one meets,
Make up my rosary, hear my confession.
These names make up my mantra I repeat,
My Japa, in my fervid state of mind
When other thoughts have all been obsolete
In guiding me, to where I am inclined.
What is this madness, Lord? What this despair
Tormenting me, and seemingly unceasing,
When all my efforts lead me to no where,
And all my burdens seem to be increasing?
Their thought, the same weird journey having taken,
Doth comfort me—that yet may be mistaken.

65

Dear reader of these poems, here is a tip
To much of what seems painful and ascetic,
My life has never been one downward slip
Into despair, although it seem phrenetic;
But simply to declare, like an hermetic
Contented in his happy isolation,
To all, that all is "simply copacetic,"
Like as a postcard from a foreign nation—
Not that it would be misrepresentation
To do so, any more than what I write,
Internal pictures of deep devastation
Where all is fever-fraught, and darkest night—
Aside from lacking in utility,
To write such stuff, I lack ability.

O ho! the Catholic Church put out a book
Revising who and who can go to heaven,
The Midnight hour is near, don't be mistook,
And when the presses rolled, it was eleven.
Great thanks to his most gracious Eminence
(I'd like to kiss his ring but not his hand)
From his esteemed, sagacious prominence
For stooping so that we may understand.
I'll have to look it up, the hoist I'm planning
To see if execution will debar
Me from those pearly gates—when you examine
In detail then you get to know how far
The Law permits, before you catch some trouble,
Or if the Church has classed you with the rabble.

Father, let me not ever ask of Thee
To live another day, another hour
Beyond what Thou already gavest me,
Despite the fear of overwhelming power.
No, let me enter in unflinchingly
Into death's jaws, if such is Thy command,
As Daniel did, and he of Galilee,
Because I trust the power of Thy hand.
Let me not ever run away in fear,
Dear Lord, although like some dumb marionette
I beg of Thy support, the danger near,
The fitful terror of the gaping threat.
Because I am a coward, and a man,
Strengthen me Lord, to help fulfill Thy plan.

Father, when I was in the large cathedral
Down in Zapopan, where I saw the cup
For all posterity behind a wall
Protected and secured, and all locked up—
A wall of glass, the cup used by the Pope
Displayed for all, dear Lord, it made me angry,
Because it seemed to me religion's dope
Of glitz for which the drab masses are hungry.
Then do they know Thee, Lord, or just the tinsel
As used to decorate Thine instruments,
When every one of us is a utensil,
An implement of Thine own exigence;
But then, on second thought, I thought that they
Thy faithful were, in spite of what I say.

What Dante did was different. Dante saw
Within his eye, the consequence of action,
And how, by process as derived of law,
Despite what we profess, despite our faction,
Despite all party, reputation, section,
Nor how vociferous, if we are false,
Superb though very low in genuflexion,
That as we sow so shall we reap; naught else.
For it is our proximity to Christ
Determines to what sphere we're relegated,
Our given talents, howso we sufficed
Each with his portion he was delegated;
Wherefore, dear Lord, my conscience never calm
Cries out unto thy Son for his sweet balm.

Deliver me, dear Lord, but not from death,
But from iniquity, the greater foe,
Because the fatal blade from out its sheath
For its appointed hour Thou dost know,
Was drawn and ready for me long ago,
That cannot fail, awaiting its release,
Its aim unfailing, where it's meant to go
As certain as a man were Damocles.
Deliver me, dear Lord, but from myself,
The sabotage within I have to fear,
My evil angel or deceitful elf
That whispers vain temptations in my ear;
Enticing words, to lull my soul asleep,
Then like a succubus, my soul to keep.

Lord, flatterers and sycophants, these are
The worst of men, because by their devices
Although in their ambitions they go far,
It is by treachery, promoting crisis.
For what are men? Men are a unity,
Cohesive as a group, dependent on
Collective freedom from impunity
Or else all trust, all brotherhood, is gone.
For, like a General, the information
That comes in from his scouts, had best be true,
In their reconnaissance, or in his station
His best decisions will be faulty too.
Like as the General, so each to each
We mortal men, must help, guide, serve, and teach.

72

For there are enemies—O doubt it not!
Though women like to make it seem as if
Self-abrogation will correct the lot,
As if demureness would correct a tiff.
No, man must fortify himself to face
The naked Devil, and to overcome
Which otherwise would be his great disgrace
The Devil's hate, but not to hate succumb.
No, he must love his enemy: 'tis hard,
To love the flagellator of thy bod,
But only love can hate's accretion ward
Away, although it hurt to take the rod.
Then, when the night of torments is acceded,
And if he lives, a woman will be needed.

Vivekananda when he was in town,
Had many words to say to us, dear Lord,
How each one as a frog is living down
Deep in a well, believing it the world.
"Sisters and brothers of America,"
Did he begin his talk of toleration,
Declaring all as subject to the law
An indivisible, united nation.
When that religious parliament was held
No wonder many people stood aghast,
An hundred years ago, as clear he spelled
Out how, in Thy great scheme, the first is last;
The meek exalted, and the high made low,
And many were amazed, to hear him so.

Thy will be done, O Lord, that was the sum
Of what he had to say, although Thy law
May strike the unaccustomed cumbersome,
Pecuniary pastimes in the way.
Lord, what do we, some arrant sinner flog
Who from our judgement's call seems to depart,
When what we see is clouded by a log
Within our eye, or worse, within the heart.
Lord, why are Jesus' words so hard to bear,
Of Christian charity to one another,
When there is no one, of the people here,
That's not my father, sister, mother, brother.
Yet he will try to calcify his clan,
In monuments and graves, for such is man.

This is the day that we remember those
Who in their country's service fought, and died,
The battle over, lain in their repose
Their memories to us a source of pride,
To shore against the never-ending tide
Of time, as doth all monument efface,
We living, they the slain on either side,
Our most exalted in the human race.
We the inheritors, our glories trace
In an unbroken line to sacrifice
Most dearly of what praise cannot replace,
Their lives, and we unworthy of such price.
The scourge of war, despite that we condemn
The vulgar cause—Lord, let us honor them.

Father, unto Thy mercy never-yielding,
These fallen, we deliver to Thy care,
Though we, the Gospel-blade forever wielding
Continue fighting, clotted in despair.
Give shelter to them, Lord, heroic souls
Defeated in what men have called a game,
Red war, that fills a body full of holes
Nor even those in tact remain the same.
"Gas, gas, quick boys," he wrote, "an ecstasy
Of fumbling"—men were calling out in lime,
But war has always been a travesty
That poets, princes, popes, have called sublime.
But it has never been a source of glory,
Pro patria, to die a death so gory.

"An I did love a soldier once, he was
Taken from me, and tears were in his eyes
At his induction; so it came to pass,
Though everybody said it was not wise.
To love a soldier—and he passed from me,
In service of some principles renowned;
We wrote, I wrote, and though we pledged to be
Faithful our love in time it was disowned.
Because I saw him turn into a man,
And turning, pass from me, a lithesome lass,
A boy when he went in, in that brief span
Become a man, who from me he did pass.
I learned that love has seldom time to tarry,
Nor ever does outlast the military."

"She swore to wait for me on my return,
And I believed her vow—I was a man,
And while I was away my thoughts would burn
Through to her photograph. I got a tan.
My skin became so dark, my head so big—
Mother and sister took me to the train,
And told me not to cry—but others did—
And I could see my Momma's face in pain.
And from the train they transferred us to God
Knows where or cares, but I came through it
    though—
It strengthened me in mind and in my bod,
And taught me what a boy did never know.
She married with my friend; but we were sent,
To where I saw—well, anyhow, we went."

"I served my country fifty years ago
At Normandy, and many of us died,
But we were able to turn back the foe
And drive him out of Europe, vilified;
The Nazi threat, though I've heard said today
That what we did was not worth fighting for,
Or dying for—so to these sayers say,
Just wait until the threat is at your door.
My son was killed in battle after me,
Hamburger Hill, that ground him up like meat,
His name is on the wall, for all to see,
With all the other names, that war did eat.
I lost great many buddies, and a son,
Who heard 'the rapid rifle's orison.'"

"My son was killed in battle, and I say
No foe however great, no awful threat
Is worth the price a mother has to pay,
To see a son cut down, her baby yet.
The son I nurtured, brought forth from my womb,
Because some evil persons in a land
So far from here, have laid him in a tomb,
Forever dead, and I don't understand.
They tell me that he died to serve his country,
And gave his life, that others may breathe free,
But this, and half a dozen reasons sundry
Can't justify their taking him from me.
Mothers, give birth to daughters, not to sons,
Nor let them feed the slaughter of the guns."

Father, this bitter cup, and if it be
Thy will that I should drink it, so I shall;
Much as our Master, nailed upon the tree
Fulfilled Thy will, vague, incontestable;
Arcane Thy will, dear Lord, to mortal men
So hard to understand, to comprehend,
So hard to face high heaven's standard when
We are but low, or all to lowness tend.
The menial world, dear Lord, is but a proof
Of our great lack of faith, our daily bread
But come by bitterly, our soul aloof
From these harsh meager tasks whereby we're fed
In body, while the soul that we retain
Yearns for its freedom, "like a god in pain."

Father, deliver me the thing I want,
A limber-bodied boy I may caress,
And proffer kisses to, obsequiant
To that great need I hereby do confess;
Not old, and having touched uncouth desire,
Pursued his lusty pleasure in extreme,
Which, like as oil added to the fire
But quickly burns away the trenchant dream;
No, rather young, and still an aspirant
To dreams of love, just like I used to be,
Before her faithlessness did my hope daunt,
And treachery a madman made of me—
This I beseech Thee, Lord, to quell my torture,
Unless it goes against my human nature.

The boundless bitterness of life today
Oppresses in extremity, dear God,
Father in heaven—please show me the way
To satisfy Thy morals, and my bod;
When both, it seems to me, wage a dispute
The one against the other, tearing me
Apart, and I remain irresolute,
Between the thing I am and what should be.
Father, and if Thy will but let me have
Self-mastery o'er that by which I'm driven,
Instead of it reducing me to slave,
Not needing any more to be forgiven
My grim pursuit of that which I do crave,
Then that—self-mastery—let it be given!

Dear God! a life as lived between extremes,
Either the one, intractable enforcement
Of chastity that's anchored to false dreams
Pretending to morality's endorsement;
Or else the opposite, abandonment
Of all pretense to individuation
In love's pursuit, to moral decrement—
These both I've known, but never mediation.
God, like as land that suffers dearth and flood
In alternating waves, thus have I been;
Either too cold, or else too hot the blood,
And never gradiation in between.
Now after years of heaven, years of hell,
My body that was strong, is but a shell.

Lord, as these fiendish knots in my long hair,
So my sad tragic lovelife, which I scoff,
But while my efforts seem to get no where,
I hesitate, no less, to cut it off.
Thou comb, thou brush, as useless in the snarl,
My fingers separate it strand by strand,
But what I do, exacerbates the gnarl,
Yet, Patience, be the guidance of my hand!
Lord, women know these matters than a man
Far better, but there's no one here to ask,
So must I, fumbling, do the best I can,
Without a woman's help to ease my task.
Lord, how she helped my clumsy fingers braid
My hair, and that the least that she allayed.

Then, weak in mind, and in my body weaker,
I think upon the love we used to have,
When everything was given to the seeker,
So much, we spent, where other people save.
But like some fatalistic falling star,
Although we fell to earth, a clump of clay,
Yet none can say we didn't travel far,
Or claim unbrilliant what we did assay.
A brief conjunction: never men and women
Were meant eternally, to never part,
So love, a clinkered shale of spent bitumen
Shall leave its traces in the human heart;
Which I memorialize for all to see,
What happened in our most amazing spree.

Yet there is not a woman anywhere
But that I find in her, a trace of thee,
As like thou wert an Aunt, although more fair,
That she did copy from the face of thee.
Yet this, I know, is but imagination,
My own ascription, thoughts wrapt-up in thee,
As people who have suffered devastation
Maintain it in their mind perpetually.
Then every image of thy face not seen,
My mind caresses, like a sacred book,
The which I write, in words a subtle sheen,
But those that know thee, recognize thy look.
And yet, all verse must fail in the attempt
To capture thee, from human law exempt.

Father, that I beseech Thee for Thine aid
Itself a travesty, and mockery
Perhaps as had been better left unsaid,
Thou knowest is, and it is plain to see;
For I could not have gotten half so far
Over the distance that hath been traversed
Thus far and hitherto, across the bar
Impeding me, and from the very first;
No, I could not have moved a half an inch,
So great was my adversity, it seemed
On setting out, when cower met with flinch,
And all was hopeless, greater reason deemed;
Hadst Thou not aided me so much already,
I had been dead wherein my course is steady.

Young man, if thou wouldst write proud
   verses strong,
Then be forewarned that what the experts say,
Not only their advice gets in the way,
But more often than not, is downright wrong.
For they will tell you that (except in song)
Words ought not be repeated, wherefore they
Consult thesauri, such as by Roget,
Which only gets them words that don't belong.
Vocabulary doesn't equal strength,
Nor so-called "style" that famous popinjay
That struts his feathers in a rich array
Of color; neither brevity nor length,
Or other suchlike measures, should be sought;
Nor much re-writing, after little thought.

Courage was thine, and wisdom, my dear friend,
Though thy sweet life was passed in urgency,
With mastery against the foe that frowned,
And mystery, in thy brief sergeancy;
Thy foe the parity that leads to hate,
Thy strength serenity that leads to might,
Although the battle boil its ferment hot,
And life considered as the briefest mote.
Gratitude thine, and that deep sympathy
As must the fiercest enemies unite,
Their wounds to salve, with deepest empathy,
Although the world may little heed, or note;
Nor bearing malice, under God's dominion,
Against the foe, in that dark lonely canyon.

91

Walt Whitman wrote, as many poets did,
Most poignantly on the emancipator
Of these United States, engaged amid
Their crisis of secession never greater,
From what was ever felt to be a scourge
Against mankind, the greatest knavery,
By men as Jefferson (but not as George)
The persevering yoke of slavery;
That ancient custom—should we say, a habit?—
That all the world has known, since in the cradle
Babe man saw something and he had to grab it,
Like scooping up a meatball with a ladle;
"Property with a soul" so-called, his chattel,
That made great engines churn, and hiss, and rattle.

The time has come, my brethren black and white,
For all to understand, that we are one,
And set the age-old fallacies aright,
To finish now what Lincoln had begun;
And even ante-Lincoln, as well proved
By words of Jefferson, and other men,
So early on who fought for what they loved
Not always winning, and would fight again.
One voice of raucous, crude vociferation
Easily thwarts the best ensemble peace;
So too self-seekers, in a well-meant nation,
Who only strive to get themselves a piece;
As get their living by rude exploitation,
And hold the rest, as hostage, on their knees.

93

On sitting down to read thy verse again,
Dear William Shakespeare, I but note how far
Beneath thy standard, my trite efforts vain
Fall short, and in their meanness humbled are.
Say it was lack of skill, because I doubt
She that I love, who is my inspiration,
Falls short of her thy verses are about,
Though my attempts to praise be denigration.
Truly a sacrilege do I commit
In trying to express her beauty plainly,
When I so brief exposure had to it,
Or had in happiness, and not disdainly;
For I myself unworthy of her love
Have proven, failing that for which I strove.

94

Truly I tell the truth when I declare
I have a simple-minded feebleness
That so encloaks my vision everywhere,
That what I write, but makes my Most seem less.
For she, whom I was blessed in the possessing
Of far outshines the murky, inky lines
In which her virtues I go on professing,
Like some world-ending madman seeing signs.
Yet I have seen in this world my world's end,
When she departed from me, truly harsh
In vowing she would be no more my friend,
Whereat I fell like one lost in a marsh.
The deep miasmal smoke forever churning
But clouds my sight, although my heart is yearning.

95

Darling, thy absence constitutes distress
In which, for solace, thee I do invoke
To play my Muse, my sorrow so to dress
In pleasant rhymes, though my emotions choke,
And stultify, excess of wanting thee
But placing them from me at some extreme
Distant position, hermits so to be
Enshrouded in the cloak of love's old dream;
To take their penance, nevermore to speak
But in obscurant fashion, making signs
Whereby their sideways meaning but doth leak
Obliquely through the pattern of my lines;
Emblazoning for all the world my bleakness,
One destitute in love, reduced to weakness.

And yet, 'tis fitting. In my service as
Thy poet, but retracing o'er the meaning
Of what love meant to me, that came to pass,
Of my dependency, and bitter weaning,
Do I provide the staunchest testament
To those of little faith, who don't believe
In love's great power; what it did and meant
Within us ere it came the time to leave.
Within us and between us, I should say,
What utter change it wrought, but most in me,
Once proud like that strong oak, but made to sway
In thy fierce breeze like palm of Florida key;
To testify, who with thee cried and laughed,
That now doth feel thy distant coolness waft.

For held I you today here in my arms,
This verse were never written, never needed,
For they who feel the brunt of courtship's harms
Have need to write; not they who have succeeded.
Dismal my lot. The days that I embraced thee,
And antecedent to that, in my youth,
Before my hope was stripped and I still chased thee,
I never wrote, and didn't care for truth.
Now, though, the truth I write's a thing misshapen,
A bent out fabrication from the past
When meaning all was lost by what did happen,
Now hammered out in verse, fiercely miscast;
That gives the lie to fragrant summer nights
Swiftly succeeded by most dreadful plights.

That fragrant summer evening, on the porch,
When love was newly kindled, hope was hot,
And we so fully confident the torch
Would burn forevermore, which it did not;
So fully confident, so foolishly—
Because we both were young, our youth not knowing,
As lovers never do, their me and thee
But all encompassing, and all endowing.
That this too soon would pass, the quick succession
Events unfolding soon would bring to bear
On what we had, did not infect our session
Of love, thought's intimation coming near.
Yet quickly both we knew contamination:
Doubt, jealousy, despair, and deprivation.

99

Tonight is calm; and while I think on thee,
My body gives a shudder through each member,
Recalling what it was to hold, and be
Held by thy slight embrace—ay, to remember.
From such derives the word "exquisite," or
For one since world-weary, "recondite,"
When I had thee and each to each was for
Love's mutual contemplation to requite.
Requite, unite! All words are utterly
Devoid of content—harking back to that
We had, now vanished as the butterfly
As lovers duly ponder, gazing at;
Like on soft summer nights, from backyard swings,
When love outstretched displays her fragile wings.

I knew some time ago that you were not
Mine though your body lingers here with me;
But I must not disparage what was fraught
Ever with debacles, to harsh degree.
So thou must go. It is as it should be,
Departing here, before the dream's eclipse
Transform into a madness killing thee
By killing me, though longing for thy lips.
The greatest grace a woman or a man
May be possessor of, is knowing when
To leave, before love has outspent its span,
Believing vainly hope may spring again.
Yet many poems have vouchsafed it is true
Love can revive; but never, lacking you.

Like as a termite, gnawing at the core
Of what I feel, the love that I confess,
There lurks a hidden doubt as does implore
My secret thought which I dare not express:
That thou art false, that thou wast ever so;
That all thy faithfulness deceitful art,
And all thy gentleness an artful show
Hath ever been, as one who plays a part.
Yet, even be it a sublime enactment
Of vain delusions, harbored by a fool,
A joke at my expense, wherein to act meant
Relinquishing my faith to torments cruel—
I'll play my part, protracting the confusion,
Possessed of thy delectable illusion.

102

My style is artificial; this be said—
Yet something underlying it there is
Approaching truth, though love forever fled
Now takes its throne in heaven's, not earth's, bliss.
Heavenly, that's a meaningless conception
Save that, to my experience profound
When I saw thee that was my love's inception,
No other word apply, myself disowned.
Heaven to which I clung with my mind blunt
Though it the rest of me consigned to hell,
A stunted reprobate, misshapen runt,
I proffer thee my thanks for what befell!
For thou hast rescued me from mine own self,
And from the restless quest for useless pelf.

Like rotted flesh with worms my dull brain teems
With thoughts of you, encompassing my night,
Long night of restlessness, devoid of dreams,
Except such as my loneliness doth write.
Truly 'tis better never to have tasted
The moist-mouthed kiss of such a love divine,
Forevermore to feel one's days as wasted
Subsequently for former love to pine.
Though I may one day find another lover
As to thee in some slight degree resembles,
Yet I may never live those gone days over,
At memory whereof my faint heart trembles.
But yet, a man can't help but reminiscing
On vanished love that he continues missing.

Los pechos redolentes I did proffer
With kisses, meeter than an idol's foot,
Of my idolatry the fragrant altar,
Two effervescent islands shimmering
Within a sea of moonlight, placid, mute,
As makes the most austere devotee falter
Before such a demure, enchanting thing,
Of all the wonders nature has to offer.
These are an easy image, well touched-on
By poets of repute since ancient time,
But even they do seem jejune, effete,
Against the glories of his port sublime
Wherein a man takes his enduring treat,
As votaries and votaries have done.

Thou nubile princess! have at it with me,
Thy graces manifold to manifest
Within my company, within the gloom
Of moonlight's pale reflection, thou disrobed
In all thy natural splendor unsuppressed,
All free, in the confinements of a room
Where we may see love's pleasant pastimes probed,
To our own natural selves, in fealty.
Thou wast, if only for this very night
Intended for my ravishing, thou wert,
In all thy nakedness, meant to be kissed
And handled in such ways as never hurt,
Thy form my shrine, that part of me so missed
That all my body's longing doth requite.

As thou wast mine, so other men may have
Love to requite them in their fervent longing,
Love that doth strangely change how we behave
Like full-moon's light, and leads us into wronging
If not in its intent then its effect,
For what is the result of love save sorrow
Except when briefly, present hearts connect
In present actions heeding no tomorrow?
So had we, in our love's brief many years
For all to see, in our contumacy
Like as against Time's crush to see our tears,
Exemption from his hand, in our wild spree.
Except that thou art in my heart entombed,
There is no trace of what here was consumed.

Father, a thousand beauties in my thrall
Would never compensate for loss of her,
Though they possessed their sex's virtues all
And not its vices, but did all defer
To codes of gracefulness, propriety
As is so lacking in our women now,
But acquiescing to whatever they
In pleasure's fast pursuit themselves allow.
Lord, did they learn from men, or men from them
In how to disabuse, exonerate
Codes of licentiousness wherefrom doth stem
Such cheap excess as kept inviolate?
No, like as not they learned it from us men;
Or maybe not, so it get taught again.

Hast dropped thy litter, pregnant Calico,
And thou a pup thyself—I see thou art
Less full in belly, which before did show
Rotund thy load, not nature's plan athwart.
So young—the neighbors seeing one depart
Its comfort's confines of thy heaving womb,
Did say of thee, "She ran off with a start
With that old Tom"—I asked who? "Old grey Tom"—
Like as to implicate thee as a mom
Unfit for child-rearing. They the kitten
Did scoop, so they did say, to take to home,
They with its weak debility all smitten.
Yet "unfit moms" so-called, are often fitter
Than high-bred dames like these to have a litter.

So life pursues its cycle, as it has
Since eons immemorial, and shall
After the final man sighs his "alas,"
And goes unto his death, as doth befall
God's creatures, high and lowly, big and small,
Forever in the workings of His eye,
Shifting its soul-filled change perpetual
As some are born while others have to die
Unceasingly—yet only man doth cry
Unto high heaven, Thine ears to abuse,
His petty loss and loves, and such am I,
A poet, mortal creature most obtuse;
Yet being so, I help fulfill Thy plan,
Thy Comedy, that is the life of man.

A comedy and tragedy it is
In selfsame time—these phrases but a frame
Through which to see most fascinating This,
Indefatigable, most free from blame,
The workings of Thine eye and holy Name
To which a man is prostrate, or before
Which denigrates himself in blame and shame,
Fearing the worst that may be yet in store.
Yet from the cringing cow-tow of the coward
Thy son, dear Lord, didst Thou send unto us,
To save us from ourselves that greed devoured,
And taught us how to bow but thus and thus.
Respectful, unto Thee obeisance paying,
Requited by Thy mercy most, most straying.

"Then go and sin no more" did Jesus say
To her indicted for adultery—
As one by one, Accusers dropped away
And they alone left standing, he and she.
What had she done, so Great to get a Grudge,
What crime committed worthy they withhold
Forgiveness, from their staunchness not to budge?
Not anything, when he stepped out so bold.
Else they would have heaped all their stones upon her,
As on the apparition of their fears,
Until the Lord so hindered what was done her—
But have we learned much, after many years?
No, even strictest, self-professing Christians
Hurl unforgiving Damns in hate-filled missions.

Lord, if I am a Christian let it be
The kind that hearkens thy command: forgive.
Not like so goddamned many who will see
Divergent viewpoints not allowed to live;
Divergent as from childhood conceptions
As they maintained, not in the forge of reason
Tested which is to say professed deceptions
And from what Jesus taught false, fallen treason
That masquerades in glib self-righteousness—
God, much as I do love the Word of Jesus,
So equally do I despise the mess
False followers who twist it so it pleases
Their petty dogmas—so do I despise
What these have made, their petty, rancid lies!

123

God, I may not be right, and surely am
Far from the truth in everything I write;
But try to be judicious who I damn,
And try to set internal shortfalls right,
Before a finger pointing at my brother,
And saying how, in this, in that, he sins,
Cruel mockery men wage on one another,
A jealous game most lost when one most wins.
Father, as ever on through life I trudge,
I beg of Thee, that never I presume
Myself so worthy as to be a judge,
Nor self exalt to higher than Thy Doom;
For though I pray that Thou deliver me,
Condemn me, Lord, if such Thy will it be.

Father, to salvage my poor wretched soul
If it be possible, I beg of Thee—
Yet I believe it is impossible,
Unless Thy mercy undeserved of be
Given me in my still strong sinfulness,
In spite of it, by which I am so driven,
Abscessed corruption all my soul to stress
Unless it by sweet mercy's lance be riven.
Father, I fear that my hypocrisy
So like a cancer, has invaded all
My spirit to the marrow thoroughly,
So thoroughly, great sorrow must befall.
Yet, so much do I fear the spirit's plagues,
I'd rather have the body torn to rags.

One must be strong; but, Father, it is hard,
So hard when all about us we observe
That falsehood and deceit seem to reward,
While truth and faith most torture that most serve.
This all have seen—and Justice only known
By its heartwrenching absence in man's world,
The ancient Confidence to heaven flown,
Or else down to the craggy hellholds hurled.
Yet, Lord, deliver me from the deserved,
For what do I deserve but death most foul?
Forgive me in that I have greatly swerved
From Thine intent, and nearly lost my soul
An hundred times, and body all unnerved—
An hundred hundred times—Lord, keep me whole!

116

In such a wretchedness naught can console—
And so, my spinning mind to slow, and steady,
Must I recall the one to whom my soul
Was consecrated, though it wasn't ready
To meet the challenges upon it thrust
In consecration—but, like any boy,
I freely gave, as would-be lovers must,
And so was led to sorrow and to joy.
This be the emblem of my victory
Which never be revealed, save soul to heart,
Against the forces fierce that threatened me
And overwhelmed me at my journey's start.
Yet, let not boastings proud my hope unravel,
When victory's far-off, and I must travel.

So onward into all-engulfing night
Must I proceed, but let me not despair,
But ever keep her memory in sight,
And trust, somehow, that it will guide me there;
There to where I was meant to end my journey,
Wherever that may be—though I have sinned
Let her sweet arguments be my attorney,
So sweet my harsher judgement to rescind.
Like men do plead for mercy on the court
Invoking matters far-flung from the case
Irrelevant, so in my poor report
Must I invoke but briefly her sweet face;
Then all who hear my lachrymose appeal
Decide, not on the facts, but what they feel.

Thou jade, hast thou revived? What jubilation
Is mine to see thy leaves so lush and fair,
So thickly green, past thy sick enervation
Brought back to life, thy healthy state's repair!
Yet this, thy gain, is only temporary,
As old Philosophers have taught and taught,
For thou must die, and meet that judgement scary
One day anon, thy soul to Maker brought.
Yet that, to this, miraculous revival,
In jubilation far shall it exceed
By its compare, that day of thine arrival
At Eden's gate, pure sinless like a seed;
Forsaking earth's corrupt, pollution-fraught
Excess and unto quietus be brought.

So he hath left thee, now thou dost return
To me, and saying that the fault was thine,
A change of heart, and showing great concern
In how my days are passed, which do repine.
My friend says stay away, that thou a shrew
Hast ever been; no sooner that doth find
Another love, will prove again untrue,
For love was ever furthest from thy mind.
This may well be, but shall I heed that friend
Who in his escapades, in equal folly
Hath acted; or my need that doesn't end
To stifle, squelch, and stop love's melancholy
As hath, since thy departure, issued from
My heart unceasingly. So then, sweet, come.

I know that it will lead to living hell
Again, but I have no defense against
Thy subtle charms, and reason cannot quell
What heart in ardency would see would see
    commenced.
O take me far from here, dear God! by plane,
Into a foreign land, so to escape
The madness now encroaching on my brain,
Old hope, new fear, a tingle at the nape.
No, no! I cannot go to where she is,
Though it was plain to me where she would be,
What she did intimate—enough of this!
I'm not a toy, that thou canst play with me!
This is what I will say, say that the past
Lies buried, mourned, not fit for fresh repast.

Like some old rancid meat, some few days old,
Not fit for fresh consumption, what we had,
Which, in the best of days, was never cold,
And in the worst of days, was not so bad.
For though we had our times of arguments,
We had our times of peaceful armistice;
Our nights when we encamped in different tents,
And nights when love was sealed with a kiss.
No, he is fit for thee, and thou for him;
For I prefer that happy memories
Retain their luster, than to let them dim
With grievances afresh, and tears' release.
No, in the early days, tears brought relief,
But now thy grievances would be my grief.

No, never anymore, to kiss thee, fair!
No, never anymore to call thy name!
To stare into the night, and wonder where,
And in whose bed thou wert, the same, the same!
Shall I relive those nights of agony,
My faithfulness to thee the joke of jokes,
Vacuous night, malignant entity
So spent in missing what was all a hoax!
The hoax of hoaxes! Man has no defense
Against thy crafty charms, thy charm which coaxes
His heart out of its casement, common sense
Subverted so to perpetrate thy hoaxes.
No, I, as never fond of Cardiff Giants,
Prefer my heart to keep its self-reliance.

My lonely heart! Why do you torment me,
Thou spectre from the past, when thy *absentia*
Which I sought to forstave on bended knee
Has been adjusted to; now new dementia
Dost thou propose, like as some sneaky thought
Inducing in my addled brain, that was
Contented in its peacefulness, not fraught
With consternation, Ghost that will not pass.
When all my feelings hurt have long been buried,
Dost thou propose to dig them up again,
My faithful hopes, that utterly miscarried,
The hoped-for joy revoked in hopeless pain.
No, I have been accustomed to unfeeling,
Instead of to and fro, forever reeling.

I say, with thee, there shall be no more dealing,
Heart's delicacy proffering, so tender,
For thou thine art hast taught me, thought-concealing,
So for thy "sweet deceit" deceit I'll render.
In thee dependency on love I'll foster,
Beguiling thee with subtle, poet's words,
In love's allegiance thou thy paternoster
Shalt say, then I'll requite thee with sharp swords.
The sharpest swords, that non-existent are,
That wound by their removal, not incision,
Love's absence cutting deeper than love's care
Was wont in its transmogrified derision.
Thus shall I scorn for scorn repay thy hate,
Withdrawing early, rather than too late.

Father, forgive me! Vengeance so to sate
But doth me little honor. So shall I
Instead in verse, what I rehearse, relate,
And her relation nevermore to try.
For she was beautiful, and I was young,
And, for a time, the world seemed at our feet;
Then let the best thoughts come to mind and
    tongue,
My angry passion's thoughts not to repeat.
Then when I see her, I shall bow to her
In courtesy, politely, as they do
In gothic novels, times such as they were;
But if she bid to me, I shall not go.
I shall not follow her, though she is good,
And though my heart is lonely, ever brood.

So shall I ever follow her, the way
I always have; but softly, from a distance,
My adulation secretly to pay,
Because it is the way of least resistance.
Lord, when we were together, we did quarrel
About such tepid, insubstantial topics
As now we both repent. Let us apparel
Our love with less of talk, as for the tropics,
Where living's easier than wintry clime,
To take our life in stride, and for the moment
Enjoy the moment's pleasures—less of crime,
Comparison, and fault to make our comment.
As in a dream, our life that opens, closes,
So let us take our time with wine and roses.

Cally, I'll let thee know, thy urchin kitten
Hath found a happy home, thy little pup,
Not that thou carest to hear, thou having bitten
The cord umbilical forever up;
And thou, so svelte, where goest thou but forth
To try the world again in its adventure,
The plenitudinous expanse thy berth,
Unlike to cats in pethood's closed indenture.
But little dost thou know my lady friend
Devises stratagems to take thee in
In all thy sweetness, wherefore to forfend
Potential harm, as cars that always win
Against small creatures as thyself; and I
Assist her in this—little cutie-pie!

For I was faithful to thee, in my fashion,
But never anymore, that kind of faith,
Will offer, nevermore that kind of passion,
To any, even the sublimest wraith.
For I was faithful to thee, this God knows,
As, likewise, all my poets, can attest
That over me did watch, through my love's throes,
For thee, for thee, through nights deprived of rest.
For though it was an accident, to love,
And though a sorrow, now to have to leave,
I lost, and there is nothing more to prove,
So why should I then struggle to believe.
Poets, my predecessors, so we all
Proceed into eternity's nightfall.

If, like that small stray cat, could I subvert thee,
Waylay thee to my house, to be the warden
Over thy love, and if it didn't hurt thee,
Then I would do so, save thy feelings harden.
For that which I did love in thee was born
Of thy strong freedom, and thy manner bold,
Although my love thou didst requite with scorn,
And, leaving, took away that I would hold.
For that is as it should be: so to guard
Thy beauty in a closet, but for me
To worship, like as though thou wert my ward,
Would wither that that thriveth being free.
No, save thy memory shall I imprison
In deep heart's core—arise what will be risen.

No, captured love, from love it must decline,
More firmly held, but sooner says goodbye,
Awhile and a day, yet thou wast mine,
And, inconceivably, thy lover, I.
Although it passed—what, was it years, or days?—
Thy brief sojourn upon my breast did last
Just long enough to garner thee my praise
Eternally, or till my life is passed.
Yes, "just so long" so said, "and long enough,"
Enough love's every promise to fulfill—
But just enough, until thy last rebuff,
To make me hunger for it even still.
Yet still, as in a dream, 'tis best to have thee
That comes and goes—than steadfastness enslave thee.

So let us linger here a while, and talk
Of what went wrong, that couldn't be made right,
Those men that loved thee, whom thou didst requite
With thine attentions, though it made me balk.
Yet, like some men, their women who do stalk
In jealousy's derangement, though I might
In mind pursue thee, yet an anchorite
I'd rather be, and with illusion walk.
For so, in my divorce from what is real,
Thy love, in some strange way, may I possess,
So linger on emotions that I feel,
And thy sweet truth to all the world profess;
Though what I write, a something must conceal
Such as the depth of loss and bitterness.

The night is hot; this summer sweltering,
Like as we never noticed, our own heat
But made the outer world seem a cold thing,
And so I dwell on thee, and so repeat
What I would say to thee, if we did meet
Again, and if the past could be re-written,
Responsive words that thou shouldst utter, sweet,
These I imagine, ever with thee smitten.
Somewhere thou art tonight, so paltry breeze
Caressing of my skin, doth softly whisper;
Somewhere thou art, not thinking thoughts as these
That make the substance of my lonely vesper.
Like as the rosary, with clack of beads,
I recollect the hours—and unmet needs.

"Son, I have brought thee here by skill, and art;
Now what thy pleasure is, to take for guide—
Having come down from that steep, narrow part
Look thou upon the sun that doth not hide;
The flowers, trees and grass, earth all-producing,
To pass thy while among them and so bide
Till those eyes beautiful do come rejoicing,
Which, weeping, me unto thy crisis hied.
Expect no further word or sign from me:
Free, upright, whole, and sane is now thy will,
And it were wrong to not act on its bidding:
Over thyself I crown and mitre thee."
Thus Virgil spoke to Dante, Dante still;
But then he went, to wait his coming chiding.

I hear that thou hast worked things out with him,
Happy am I for thee, must I confess,
For he is worthy of thee, if thy whim
To his true protestations answers yes;
For he is good, and if not faithful, true;
Well-versed in worldly things far-flung from verse;
And I contented with the residue
Thy love hath left for fame, where it inheres.
Happy am I with what thou hast bequeathed me,
A flagon full of memories most fine,
For which, reiterating, men may wreath me
With laurel, though their tribute all is thine.
For I had scant occasion to invent,
Since what I write remains what thou hast lent.

135

Thy poet I shall be; and he, thy love—
It is a just division of man's labors,
For he finite in thee, while I must rove
Over the world, in search of pipes and tabors.
As Michelangelo was married to
His art, so he did say, let me be wed
To this my craft, forever to pursue
Thy charms but not to ever share thy bed.
Beauty hast thou, in such a magnitude,
Refined, so very subtle, it would take
Of scribblers centuries, and then a brood
To write it all, and too their hearts would break.
My life to thee forever consecrate,
In verse thy power I delineate.

Enough of this! my twisty-wisty phrases,
All syntax-broke, and taking leave of grammar,
Ill-suited to describe thy love's sweet phases,
Love eloquent, when I at best but stammer.
Like something that is wrought out with a hammer,
(Look, there's the cleft-mark where the chisel struck!)
Describing thee in words bereft of glamour—
A better poet ought to try his luck!
For I, illiterate, unlettered am,
A fool with a vocabulary, drifting
Lone on an ocean, with no diagram
To teach me, so through words I keep on sifting.
Words, words, to me a shiftless, clanging clamor,
Since, having known thee, they cannot enamor.

So while I muse my secret thoughts out-loud,
In barbarous tongue, so ill-befitting thee
Of whom I write, that hast been so out-thou'd,
No wonder there be no requiting me;
Thee, thou, and thine, instead of you and yours,
But words to keep thee from me far apart,
So sacred cherished what from me outpours
Because, to hold thee nearer, hurts my heart.
Thus thou, and thine, since words were never pleasing
To thee, to you, as did thy scorn provoke,
Once proffered, herewith laid ope to thy teasing,
Such ridicule as thou dost care to poke.
And yet, to beat the old tale black and blue,
The only thou I ever loved was you.

138

So I and thou, it could be me and you,
Kiddo, but that was once, and might have been,
But this is now, and I forever true
Could not have been, in light of what I've seen.
For I have seen, abjectly, the reversal
Of every thought I thought I ever had,
My empty bag now scattered for dispersal,
Its contents mostly good when they are bad.
So furthermore, on thee I lavish praise
To mock myself, that is cheap counterfeit
Of thee, derived from thee, whom I always
Do plunder for my thought's unlettered writ.
So, so it goes. Thou reader, stand unfazed:
For if you saw her face, you'd be amazed.

139

Father, as he his verses did retract
Who wrote the tales of Canterbury, I
Should do, would do, except the mordant fact
That she made me a poet; so I try
Something of what I've seen, what I have known,
To set down in my verse for all to see,
Though for the reading of such men have gone
So errantly astray; and worse, from Thee.
Lord, these to all the world do I present,
But if a syllable should cause a servant
Of Thine to lose his way, by accident,
Forgive me, Lord; because my love was fervent.
Love that so utterly did see me ruined,
Wherefore Thy mercy have I importuned.

God, let me hold my tongue, and now be mute
Forevermore, unless it be Thy will
That I should all the world tell her repute
Again, again, its poor sad ear to fill.
Harangued, the world has had enough of love,
Enough and not enough, of foolish whining
As done by poets, human hearts to move
Which all alike have shared in love's repining.
That Thou hast carried me in my sad quest
This far, and having nearly had fulfillment
In that for which I strove at love's behest
Attests Thy mercy's solace in my ailment.
Father, I fell in love, and ever since
My life had meaning; please forgive my sins.

Index of First Lines

About the Author

David Novak was born in 1962 in Elmhurst, Illinois. He graduated from Mundelein College with a focus in Spanish literature and later studied Chinese in Taipei, Taiwan. Since 1986 he has lived in Chicago, where he studied voice and dance and helped stage productions by several local opera companies, serving in positions ranging from technical assistant to stage manager. This involvement with theater led him to write *Titus Androgynous*, the first of nine verse plays. He is also the author of two collections of poetry, *Embodiment and Release* and *The Soul's Refinement*. His epic poem, *The Requiem*, was published by Non Fit Press in 1999.